KNIT STITCH:
50 KNIT + PURL PATTERNS

Created by Kristen McDonnell

production • knitting • photography

art direction • cover design • layout • text

© StudioKnit LLC 2019

www.StudioKnitSF.com

WELCOME!

As the creator of Studio Knit, I want to personally thank you for supporting my work as an independent knitting teacher.

This book is a companion to my online video tutorials found on my Studio Knit website and YouTube. Enjoy selecting among my fun collection of favorite vintage knit and purl stitch textures. These written and charted patterns will help you design scarves, blankets, dishcloths, and more.

I hope you are inspired to knit up the perfect for knitters of all levels!

ABOUT THIS PATTERN BOOK

This Knit Stitch Pattern Book gives you 50 unique hand-knit stitch patterns. These are all great for beginning knitters since they use only the simplest knit and purl stitch techniques.

Large color photos help you envision each texture while designing your own knitting projects. Easily understand exactly how to create each texture stitch-by-stitch with chart diagrams and written instructions to knit both flat and in the round.

ROW REPEATS

Patterns in this book are organized by their row repeats, beginning with the simplest 2-row repeats and advancing up to more intricate 28-row repeats.

Example: 4-row repeat instructions. Once you knit rows 1 to 4, begin again with row 1 ending with row 4 until you piece is the length you desire.

KNITTING TECHNIQUES

Slip Knot	K = Knit Stitch	Bind Off
Cast On	P = Purl Stitch	Weave In Ends

CASTING ON

Cast On instructions allow you to cast on as many stitches as you wish to have for each row.

Example: Casting on in multiples of 4 would be any number of stitches that are divisible by 4, such as 8, 16, 24, etc. When casting on in multiples plus another number, such as 4 plus 2, you will first cast on in multiples of 4, then add 2 extra stitches at the very end.

WRITTEN INSTRUCTIONS

 NOT REVERSIBLE
Design on Right Side

 REVERSIBLE
Design on Both Sides

All patterns begin with odd numbered rows as the Right Side of the work. Stitch repeats are indicated as underlined and between asterisks.

Example: * K4, P2 *, K4
Knit 4 stitches, then Purl 2 stitches. Repeat this pattern all the way down your needle until you have 4 stitches remaining and knit those last 4 stitches. When you are knitting back and forth on straight knitting needles, you are knitting "Flat." When using circular knitting needle for projects like hats, you are knitting "In The Round."

READING CHARTS

Knitting Charts allow you to knit without referring to the written instructions laid out in a grid. That grid has little cells, like an Excel document or graph paper. Each of those boxes represents one stitch on your needle. The entirety of the chart represents your knitting pattern.

Chart symbols are included on each page for reference.

RS = Right Side (odd # rows)
WS = Wrong Side (even # rows)

| | RS: Knit WS: Purl | ● | RS: Purl WS: Knit |

Grayed out chart areas indicate the extra stitches after row repeat multiples.

Each chart can be read for both "Flat" and "In The Round" projects. When knitting flat, begin reading the chart right to left on the odd (right sides) of your work, then read left to right on the even (wrong sides). When knitting in the round, read the chart right to left for all rows of your project.

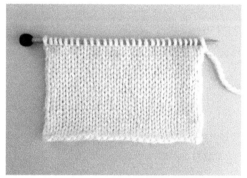

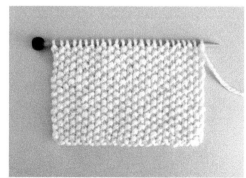

1

2-ROW REPEATS

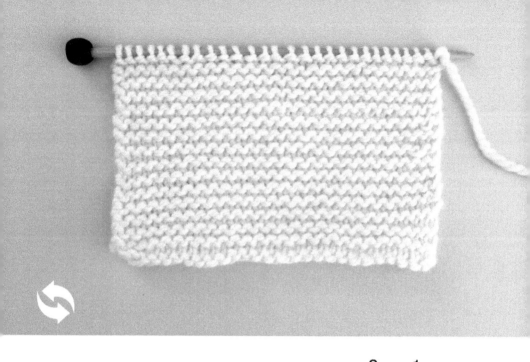

GARTER

CAST ON

Any Number of Stitches

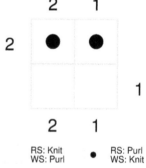

RS: Knit
WS: Purl

● RS: Purl
WS: Knit

FLAT

Row 1: Knit All

Row 2: Knit All

IN THE ROUND

Row 1: Knit All

Row 2: Purl All

STOCKINETTE

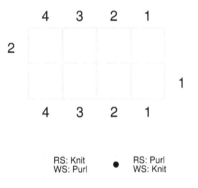

	4	3	2	1	
2					
					1
	4	3	2	1	

RS: Knit
WS: Purl

● RS: Purl
WS: Knit

CAST ON

Any Number of Stitches

FLAT

Row 1: Knit All

Row 2: Purl All

IN THE ROUND

Row 1: Knit All

Row 2: Knit All

1x1 RIB

CAST ON

Multiples of 2

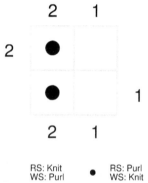

	2	1
2	●	
	●	1
	2	1

RS: Knit
WS: Purl

● RS: Purl
WS: Knit

FLAT

Row 1: * <u>K1, P1</u> *

Row 2: * <u>K1, P1</u> *

IN THE ROUND

Row 1: * <u>K1, P1</u> *

Row 2: * <u>K1, P1</u> *

2x2 RIB

CAST ON

Multiples of 4

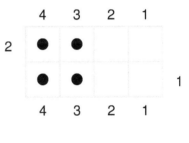

	4	3	2	1	
2	●	●			
	●	●			1
	4	3	2	1	

RS: Knit
WS: Purl

● RS: Purl
WS: Knit

FLAT

Row 1: * <u>K2, P2</u> *

Row 2: * <u>K2, P2</u> *

IN THE ROUND

Row 1: * <u>K2, P2</u> *

Row 2: * <u>K2, P2</u> *

5x1 FLAT RIB

CAST ON

Multiples of 6

6	5	4	3	2	1	
●						2
●						1
6	5	4	3	2	1	

RS: Knit / WS: Purl	● RS: Purl / WS: Knit

FLAT

Row 1: * K5, P1 *

Row 2: * K1, P5 *

IN THE ROUND

Row 1: * K5, P1 *

Row 2: * K5, P1 *

7x3 FLAT RIB

CAST ON

Multiples of 10

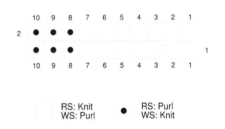

	10	9	8	7	6	5	4	3	2	1	
2	●	●	●								
	●	●	●								1
	10	9	8	7	6	5	4	3	2	1	

	RS: Knit WS: Purl	●	RS: Purl WS: Knit

FLAT

Row 1: * K7, P3 *

Row 2: * K3, P7 *

IN THE ROUND

Row 1: * K7, P3 *

Row 2: * K7, P3 *

SEED STITCH

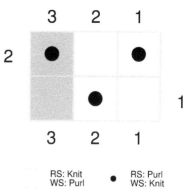

	3	2	1
2	●		●
		●		1

3   2   1

RS: Knit
WS: Purl

● RS: Purl
WS: Knit

CAST ON

Any odd number of stitches

FLAT

Row 1: * <u>K1, P1</u> *, K1

Row 2: K1, * <u>P1, K1</u> *

IN THE ROUND

Row 1: * <u>K1, P1</u> *, K1

Row 2: * <u>P1, K1</u> *, P1

GARTER RIBBING

CAST ON

Multiple of 4, plus 2

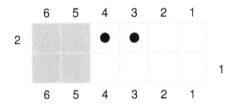

	6	5	4	3	2	1	
2			●	●			
							1
	6	5	4	3	2	1	

RS: Knit
WS: Purl

● RS: Purl
WS: Knit

FLAT

Row 1: Knit All

Row 2: P2, * <u>K2, P2</u> *

IN THE ROUND

Row 1: Knit All

Row 2: * <u>K2, P2</u> *, K2

BROKEN RIB

CAST ON

Multiples of 2, plus 1

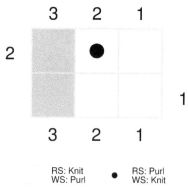

	3	2	1
2		●	
			1
	3	2	1

RS: Knit
WS: Purl

● RS: Purl
WS: Knit

FLAT

Row 1: Knit All

Row 2: * <u>P1, K1</u> *, P1

IN THE ROUND

Row 1: Knit All

Row 2: * <u>K1, P1</u> *, K1

SAND STITCH

CAST ON

Multiples of 2, plus 1

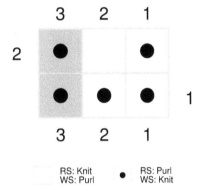

RS: Knit
WS: Purl

● RS: Purl
WS: Knit

FLAT

Row 1: Purl All

Row 2: K1, * P1, K1 *

IN THE ROUND

Row 1: Purl All

Row 2: * P1, K1 *, P1

BEADED RIB

CAST ON

Multiples of 5, plus 2

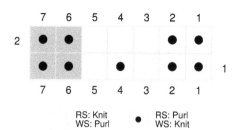

	7	6	5	4	3	2	1	
2	●	●				●	●	
	●	●		●		●	●	1
	7	6	5	4	3	2	1	

RS: Knit
WS: Purl

● RS: Purl
WS: Knit

FLAT

Row 1: * <u>P2, K1, P1,</u>
<u>K1</u> *, P2

Row 2: K2, * <u>P3, K2</u> *

IN THE ROUND

Row 1: * <u>P2, K1, P1,</u>
<u>K1</u> *, P2

Row 2: * <u>P2, K3</u> *, P2

SEEDED RIB

CAST ON

Multiples of 4, plus 3

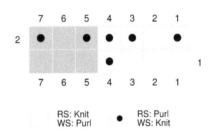

	7	6	5	4	3	2	1	
2	●		●	●		●		
				●				1
	7	6	5	4	3	2	1	

RS: Knit
WS: Purl

● RS: Purl
WS: Knit

FLAT

Row 1: * <u>K3, P1</u> *, K3

Row 2: K1, P1, K1,

    * <u>K2, P1, K1</u> *

IN THE ROUND

Row 1: * <u>K3, P1</u> *, K3

Row 2: * <u>P1, K1, P2</u> *,

    P1, K1, P1

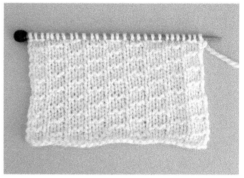

4-ROW REPEATS

ANDALUSIAN

CAST ON

Multiples of 2, plus 1

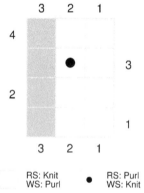

RS: Knit
WS: Purl

● RS: Purl
WS: Knit

FLAT

Row 1: Knit All

Row 2: Purl All

Row 3: * <u>K1, P1</u> *, K1

Row 4: Purl All

IN THE ROUND

Row 1: Knit All

Row 2: Knit All

Row 3: * <u>K1, P1</u> *, K1

Row 4: Knit All

CHEVRON SEED

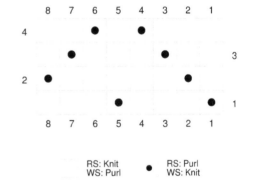

8	7	6	5	4	3	2	1	
		●		●				4
	●				●			3
●					●			2
			●				●	1

RS: Knit
WS: Purl

● RS: Purl
WS: Knit

CAST ON

Multiples of 8

FLAT

Row 1: * <u>P1, K3, P1, K3</u> *

Row 2: * <u>K1, P5, K1, P1</u> *

Row 3: * <u>K2, P1, K3, P1, K1</u> *

Row 4: * <u>P2, K1, P1, K1, P3</u> *

IN THE ROUND

Row 1: * <u>P1, K3, P1, K3</u> *

Row 2: * <u>K1, P1, K5, P1</u> *

Row 3: * <u>K2, P1, K3, P1, K1</u> *

Row 4: * <u>K3, P1, K1, P1, K2</u> *

DOUBLE FLECK

CAST ON

Multiples of 6, plus 4

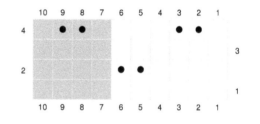

FLAT

Row 1: Knit All

Row 2: P4, * K2, P4 *

Row 3: Knit All

Row 4: P1, K2, P1,

　　　* P3, K2, P1 *

IN THE ROUND

Row 1: Knit All

Row 2: * K4, P2 *, K4

Row 3: Knit All

Row 4: * K1, P2, K3 *,

　　　K1, P2, K1

DOUBLE MOSS

CAST ON

Multiples of 4, plus 2

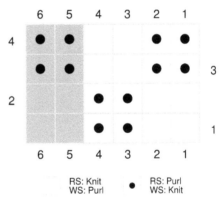

RS: Knit
WS: Purl

● RS: Purl
WS: Knit

FLAT

Row 1: * <u>K2, P2</u> *, K2

Row 2: P2, * <u>K2, P2</u> *

Row 3: * <u>P2, K2</u> *, P2

Row 4: K2, * <u>P2, K2</u> *

IN THE ROUND

Row 1: * <u>K2, P2</u> *, K2

Row 2: * <u>K2, P2</u> *, K2

Row 3: * <u>P2, K2</u> *, P2

Row 4: * <u>P2, K2</u> *, P2

HURDLE

CAST ON

Multiples of 2

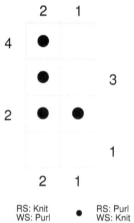

	2	1
4	●	
	●	3
2	●	●
		1
	2	1

RS: Knit
WS: Purl

●

RS: Purl
WS: Knit

FLAT

Row 1: Knit All

Row 2: Knit All

Row 3: * K1, P1 *

Row 4: * K1, P1 *

IN THE ROUND

Row 1: Knit All

Row 2: Purl All

Row 3: * K1, P1 *

Row 4: * K1, P1 *

IRISH MOSS

CAST ON

Multiples of 2

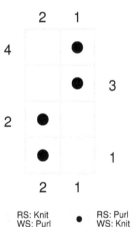

	2	1	
4		●	
		●	3
2	●		
	●		1
	2	1	

RS: Knit
WS: Purl

● RS: Purl
WS: Knit

FLAT

Row 1: * <u>K1, P1</u> *

Row 2: * <u>K1, P1</u> *

Row 3: * P<u>1, K1</u> *

Row 4: * <u>P1, K1</u> *

IN THE ROUND

Row 1: * <u>K1, P1</u> *

Row 2: * <u>K1, P1</u> *

Row 3: * P<u>1, K1</u> *

Row 4: * <u>P1, K1</u> *

PURL RIDGE

CAST ON

Any number of stitches

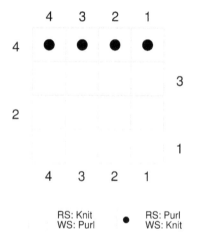

	4	3	2	1	
4	●	●	●	●	
					3
2					
					1
	4	3	2	1	

RS: Knit
WS: Purl

● RS: Purl
WS: Knit

FLAT

Row 1: Knit All

Row 2: Purl All

Row 3: Knit All

Row 4: Knit All

IN THE ROUND

Row 1: Knit All

Row 2: Knit All

Row 3: Knit All

Row 4: Purl All

PIQUE RIB

CAST ON

Multiples of 3, plus 2

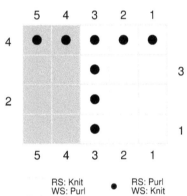

RS: Knit
WS: Purl

● RS: Purl
WS: Knit

FLAT

Row 1: * <u>K2, P1</u> *, K2

Row 2: P2, * <u>K1, P2</u> *

Row 3: * <u>K2, P1</u> *, K2

Row 4: Knit All

IN THE ROUND

Row 1: * <u>K2, P1</u> *, K2

Row 2: * <u>K2, P1</u> *, K2

Row 3: * <u>K2, P1</u> *, K2

Row 4: Purl All

WAFFLE

CAST ON

Multiples of 3, plus 1

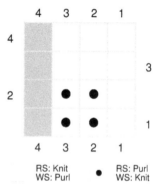

	4	3	2	1	
4					4
					3
2		●	●		2
		●	●		1
	4	3	2	1	

RS: Knit
WS: Purl

● RS: Purl
WS: Knit

FLAT

Row 1: * <u>K1, P2</u> *, K1

Row 2: P1, * <u>K2, P1</u> *

Row 3: Knit All

Row 4: Purl All

IN THE ROUND

Row 1: * <u>K1, P2</u> *, K1

Row 2: * <u>K1, P2</u> *, K1

Row 3: Knit All

Row 4: Knit All

LITTLE RAINDROPS

CAST ON

Multiples of 4, plus 3

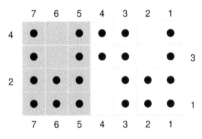

RS: Knit
WS: Purl

• RS: Purl
WS: Knit

FLAT

Row 1: * P3, K1 *, P3

Row 2: K3, * P1, K3 *

Row 3: * P1, K1, P2 *,
P1, K1, P1

Row 4: K1, P1, K1,
* K2, P1, K1 *

IN THE ROUND

Row 1: * P3, K1 *, P3

Row 2: * P3, K1 *, P3

Row 3: * P1, K1, P2 *,
P1, K1, P1

Row 4: * P1, K1, P2 *,
P1, K1, P1

6 to 10-ROW
REPEATS

FLAG STITCH

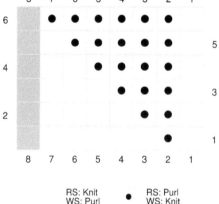

	8	7	6	5	4	3	2	1	
6		●	●	●	●	●	●		
			●	●	●	●	●	●	5
4				●	●	●	●	●	
					●	●	●	●	3
2						●	●	●	
							●	●	1
	8	7	6	5	4	3	2	1	

RS: Knit
WS: Purl

● RS: Purl
WS: Knit

CAST ON

Multiples of 7, plus 1

FLAT

Row 1: * <u>K1, P1, K5</u> *, K1

Row 2: P1, * <u>P4, K2, P1</u> *

Row 3: * <u>K1, P3, K3</u> *, K1

Row 4: P1, * <u>P2, K4, P1</u> *

Row 5: * <u>K1, P5, K1</u> *, K1

Row 6: P1, * <u>K6, P1</u> *

IN THE ROUND

Row 1: * <u>K1, P1, K5</u> *, K1

Row 2: * <u>K1, P2, K4</u> *, K1

Row 3: * <u>K1, P3, K3</u> *, K1

Row 4: * <u>K1, P4, K2</u> *, K1

Row 5: * <u>K1, P5, K1</u> *, K1

Row 6: * <u>K1, P6</u> *, K1

REVERSE RIDGE

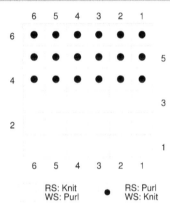

	6	5	4	3	2	1	
6	●	●	●	●	●	●	
	●	●	●	●	●	●	5
4	●	●	●	●	●	●	
							3
2							
							1
	6	5	4	3	2	1	

RS: Knit
WS: Purl
● RS: Purl
WS: Knit

CAST ON

Any number of stitches

FLAT

Row 1: Knit All

Row 2: Purl All

Row 3: Knit All

Row 4: Knit All

Row 5: Purl All

Row 6: Knit All

IN THE ROUND

Row 1: Knit All

Row 2: Knit All

Row 3: Knit All

Row 4: Purl All

Row 5: Purl All

Row 6: Purl All

TILE SQUARES

CAST ON

Multiple of 5, plus 4

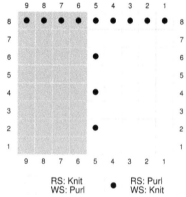

RS: Knit
WS: Purl

● RS: Purl
WS: Knit

FLAT

Row 1: Knit All
Row 2: P4, * K1, P4 *
Row 3: Knit All
Row 4: P4, * K1, P4 *
Row 5: Knit All
Row 6: P4, * K1, P4 *
Row 7: Knit All
Row 8: Knit All

IN THE ROUND

Row 1: Knit All
Row 2: * K4, P1 *, K4
Row 3: Knit All
Row 4: * K4, P1 *, K4
Row 5: Knit All
Row 6: * K4, P1 *, K4
Row 7: Knit All
Row 8: Purl All

DIAGONAL SEED

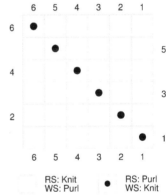

	6	5	4	3	2	1	
6	●						
		●					5
4			●				
				●			3
2					●		
						●	1
	6	5	4	3	2	1	

☐ RS: Knit
WS: Purl

● RS: Purl
WS: Knit

CAST ON

Multiple of 6

FLAT

Row 1: * P1, K5 *

Row 2: * P4, K1, P1 *

Row 3: * K2, P1, K3 *

Row 4: * P2, K1, P3 *

Row 5: * K4, P1, K1 *

Row 6: * K1, P5 *

IN THE ROUND

Row 1: * P1, K5 *

Row 2: * K1, P1, K4 *

Row 3: * K2, P1, K3 *

Row 4: * K3, P1, K2 *

Row 5: * K4, P1, K1 *

Row 6: * K5, P1 *

DIAGONAL RIB

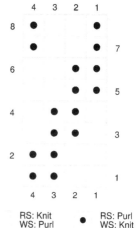

	4	3	2	1	
8	●			●	
	●			●	7
6			●	●	
			●	●	5
4		●	●		
		●	●		3
2	●	●			
	●	●			1
	4	3	2	1	

RS: Knit
WS: Purl

● RS: Purl
WS: Knit

CAST ON

Multiples of 4

FLAT

Row 1: * K2, P2 *
Row 2: * K2, P2 *
Row 3: * K1, P2, K1 *
Row 4: * P1, K2, P1 *
Row 5: * P2, K2 *
Row 6: * P2, K2 *
Row 7: * P1, K2, P1 *
Row 8: * K1, P2, K1 *

IN THE ROUND

Row 1: * K2, P2 *
Row 2: * K2, P2 *
Row 3: * K1, P2, K1 *
Row 4: * K1, P2, K1 *
Row 5: * P2, K2 *
Row 6: * P2, K2 *
Row 7: * P1, K2, P1 *
Row 8: * P1, K2, P1 *

LONG RAIN DROPS

CAST ON

Multiples of 2

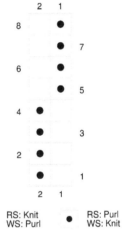

RS: Knit
WS: Purl

● RS: Purl
WS: Knit

FLAT

Row 1: * <u>K1, P1</u> *
Row 2: * <u>K1, P1</u> *
Row 3: * <u>K1, P1</u> *
Row 4: * <u>K1, P1</u> *
Row 5: * <u>P1, K1</u> *
Row 6: * <u>P1, K1</u> *
Row 7: * <u>P1, K1</u> *
Row 8: * <u>P1, K1</u> *

IN THE ROUND

Row 1: * <u>K1, P1</u> *
Row 2: * <u>K1, P1</u> *
Row 3: * <u>K1, P1</u> *
Row 4: * <u>K1, P1</u> *
Row 5: * <u>P1, K1</u> *
Row 6: * <u>P1, K1</u> *
Row 7: * <u>P1, K1</u> *
Row 8: * <u>P1, K1</u> *

PENNANT PLEATING

CAST ON

Multiples of 6

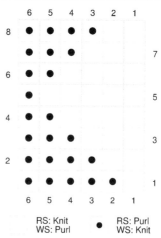

	6	5	4	3	2	1	
8	●	●	●	●			
	●	●	●				7
6	●	●					
	●						5
4	●	●					
	●	●	●				3
2	●	●	●	●			
	●	●	●	●	●		1
	6	5	4	3	2	1	

RS: Knit
WS: Purl   ●   RS: Purl
WS: Knit

FLAT

Row 1: * <u>K1, P5</u> *
Row 2: * <u>K4, P2</u> *
Row 3: * <u>K3, P3</u> *
Row 4: * <u>K2, P4</u> *
Row 5: * <u>K5, P1</u> *
Row 6: * <u>K2, P4</u> *
Row 7: * <u>K3, P3</u> *
Row 8: * <u>K4, P2</u> *

IN THE ROUND

Row 1: * <u>K1, P5</u> *
Row 2: * <u>K2, P4</u> *
Row 3: * <u>K3, P3</u> *
Row 4: * <u>K4, P2</u> *
Row 5: * <u>K5, P1</u> *
Row 6: * <u>K4, P2</u> *
Row 7: * <u>K3, P3</u> *
Row 8: * <u>K2, P4</u> *

SIMPLE SEED

CAST ON

Multiples of 4

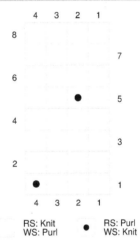

	4	3	2	1	
8					
					7
6					
			●		5
4					
					3
2					
	●				1
	4	3	2	1	

RS: Knit
WS: Purl

● RS: Purl
WS: Knit

FLAT

Row 1: * K3, P1 *
Row 2: Purl All
Row 3: Knit All
Row 4: Purl All
Row 5: * K1, P1, K2 *
Row 6: Purl All
Row 7: Knit All
Row 8: Purl All

IN THE ROUND

Row 1: * K3, P1 *
Row 2: Knit All
Row 3: Knit All
Row 4: Knit All
Row 5: * K1, P1, K2 *
Row 6: Knit All
Row 7: Knit All
Row 8: Knit All

CHEVRON RIB

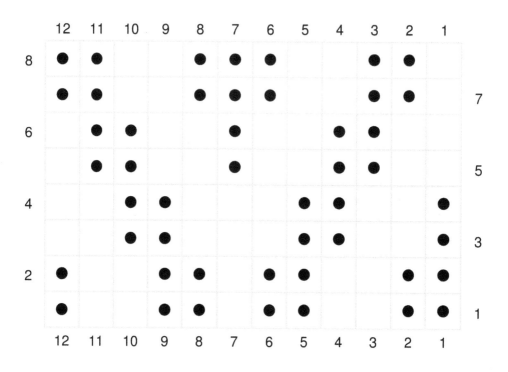

	12	11	10	9	8	7	6	5	4	3	2	1	
8	●	●			●	●	●			●	●		
	●	●			●	●	●			●	●		7
6		●	●			●			●	●			
		●	●			●			●	●			5
4			●	●				●	●			●	
			●	●				●	●			●	3
2	●			●	●		●	●			●	●	
	●			●	●		●	●			●	●	1
	12	11	10	9	8	7	6	5	4	3	2	1	

	RS: Knit	●	RS: Purl
	WS: Purl		WS: Knit

37

CHEVRON
RIB

CAST ON

Multiples of 12

FLAT

Row 1: * P2, K2, P2,
K1, P2, K2, P1 *

Row 2: * K1, P2, K2, P1,
K2, P2, K2 *

Row 3: * P1, K2, P2, K3,
P2, K2 *

Row 4: * P2, K2, P3, K2,
P2, K1 *

Row 5: * K2, P2, K2, P1,
K2, P2, K1 *

Row 6: * P1, K2, P2, K1,
P2, K2, P2 *

Row 7: * K1, P2, K2, P3,
K2, P2 *

Row 8: * K2, P2, K3, P2,
K2, P1 *

IN THE ROUND

Row 1: * P2, K2, P2, K1,
P2, K2, P1 *

Row 2: * P2, K2, P2, K1,
P2, K2, P1 *

Row 3: * P1, K2, P2, K3,
P2, K2 *

Row 4: * P1, K2, P2, K3,
P2, K2 *

Row 5: * K2, P2, K2, P1,
K2, P2, K1 *

Row 6: * K2, P2, K2, P1,
K2, P2, K1 *

Row 7: * K1, P2, K2, P3,
K2, P2 *

Row 8: * K1, P2, K2, P3,
K2, P2 *

DIAMOND BROCADE

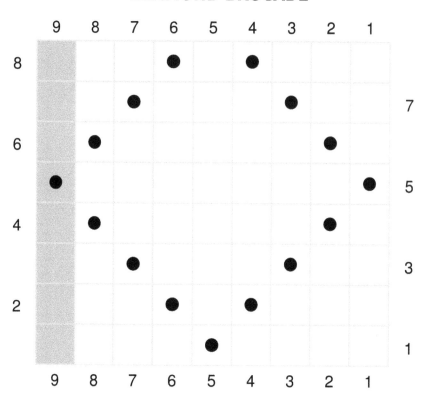

	9	8	7	6	5	4	3	2	1	
8				●		●				
			●				●			7
6		●						●		
	●								●	5
4		●					●			
			●				●			3
2				●		●				
					●					1
	9	8	7	6	5	4	3	2	1	

	RS: Knit	●	RS: Purl
	WS: Purl		WS: Knit

DIAMOND
BROCADE

CAST ON

Multiples of 8, plus 1

FLAT	IN THE ROUND
Row 1: * K4, P1, K3 *, K1	**Row 1:** * K4, P1, K3 *, K1
Row 2: P1, * P2, K1, P1, K1, P3 *	**Row 2:** * K3, P1, K1, P1, K2 *, K1
Row 3: * K2, P1, K3, P1, K1 *, K1	**Row 3:** * K2, P1, K3, P1, K1 *, K1
Row 4: P1, * K1, P5, K1, P1 *	**Row 4:** * K1, P1, K5, P1 *, K1
Row 5: * P1, K7 *, K1	**Row 5:** * P1, K7 *, K1
Row 6: P1, * K1, P5, K1, P1 *	**Row 6:** * K1, P1, K5, P1 *, K1
Row 7: * K2, P1, K3, P1, K1 *, K1	**Row 7:** * K2, P1, K3, P1, K1 *, K1
Row 8: P1, * P2, K1, P1, K1, P3 *	**Row 8:** * K3, P1, K1, P1, K2 *, K1

SEERSUCKER STITCH

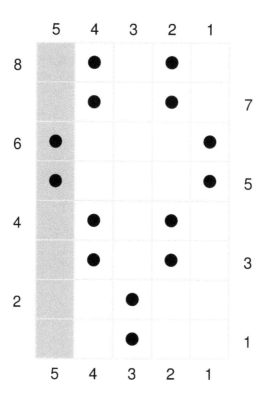

RS: Knit
WS: Purl

● RS: Purl
WS: Knit

SEERSUCKER STITCH

CAST ON

Multiples of 4, plus 1

FLAT

Row 1: * K2, P1, K1 *, K1

Row 2: P1, * P1, K1, P2 *

Row 3: * K1, P1 *, K1

Row 4: P1, * K1, P1 *

Row 5: * P1, K3 *, P1

Row 6: K1, * P3, K1 *

Row 7: * K1, P1 *, K1

Row 8: P1, * K1, P1 *

IN THE ROUND

Row 1: * K2, P1, K1 *, K1

Row 2: * K2, P1, K1 *, K1

Row 3: * K1, P1 *, K1

Row 4: * K1, P1 *, K1

Row 5: * P1, K3 *, P1

Row 6: * P1, K3 *, P1

Row 7: * K1, P1 *, K1

Row 8: * K1, P1 *, K1

Note: Repeat Rows 1 through 8 until your piece is the length you desire. Then finish your last 2 rows by repeating Rows 1 and 2.

WIDE BASKET WEAVE

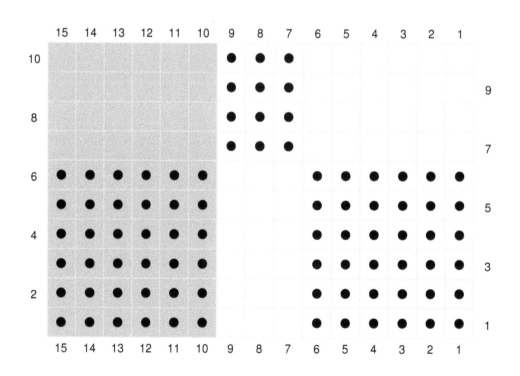

WIDE
BASKET WEAVE

CAST ON

Multiples of 9, plus 6

FLAT	IN THE ROUND
Row 1: * P6, K3 *, P6	**Row 1:** * P6, K3 *, P6
Row 2: K6, * P3, K6 *	**Row 2:** * P6, K3 *, P6
Row 3: * P6, K3 *, P6	**Row 3:** * P6, K3 *, P6
Row 4: K6, * P3, K6 *	**Row 4:** * P6, K3 *, P6
Row 5: * P6, K3 *, P6	**Row 5:** * P6, K3 *, P6
Row 6: K6, * P3, K6 *	**Row 6:** * P6, K3 *, P6
Row 7: * K6, P3 *, K6	**Row 7:** * K6, P3 *, K6
Row 8: P6, * K3, P6 *	**Row 8:** * K6, P3 *, K6
Row 9: * K6, P3 *, K6	**Row 9:** * K6, P3 *, K6
Row 10: P6, * K3, P6 *	**Row 10:** * K6, P3 *, K6

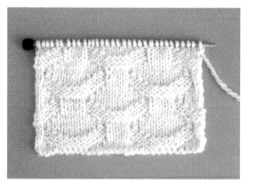

12 to 16-ROW REPEATS

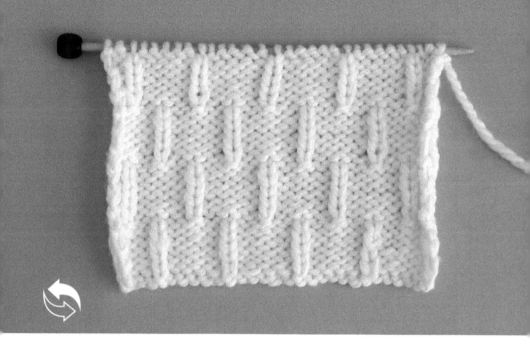

CATERPILLAR STITCH

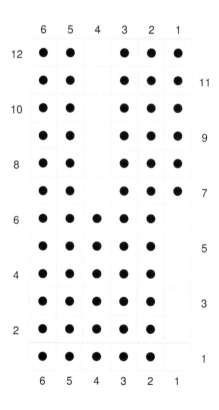

RS: Knit
WS: Purl

● RS: Purl
WS: Knit

CATERPILLAR STITCH

CAST ON

Multiples of 6

FLAT

Row 1: * K1, P5 *

Row 2: * K5, P1 *

Row 3: * K1, P5 *

Row 4: * K5, P1 *

Row 5: * K1, P5 *

Row 6: * K5, P1 *

Row 7: * P3, K1, P2 *

Row 8: * K2, P1, K3 *

Row 9: * P3, K1, P2 *

Row 10: * K2, P1, K3 *

Row 11: * P3, K1, P2 *

Row 12: * K2, P1, K3 *

IN THE ROUND

Row 1: * K1, P5 *

Row 2: * K1, P5 *

Row 3: * K1, P5 *

Row 4: * K1, P5 *

Row 5: * K1, P5 *

Row 6: * K1, P5 *

Row 7: * P3, K1, P2 *

Row 8: * P3, K1, P2 *

Row 9: * P3, K1, P2 *

Row 10: * P3, K1, P2 *

Row 11: * P3, K1, P2 *

Row 12: * P3, K1, P2 *

CLASSIC BASKET WEAVE

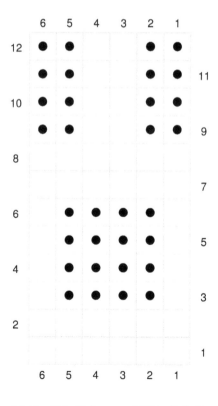

RS: Knit
WS: Purl

● RS: Purl
WS: Knit

CLASSIC
BASKET WEAVE

CAST ON

Multiples of 6

FLAT	IN THE ROUND
Row 1: Knit All	**Row 1:** Knit All
Row 2: Purl All	**Row 2:** Knit All
Row 3: * K1, P4, K1 *	**Row 3:** * K1, P4, K1 *
Row 4: * P1, K4, P1 *	**Row 4:** * K1, P4, K1 *
Row 5: * K1, P4, K1 *	**Row 5:** * K1, P4, K1 *
Row 6: * P1, K4, P1 *	**Row 6:** * K1, P4, K1 *
Row 7: Knit All	**Row 7:** Knit All
Row 8: Purl All	**Row 8:** Knit All
Row 9: * P2, K2, P2 *	**Row 9:** * P2, K2, P2 *
Row 10: * K2, P2, K2 *	**Row 10:** * P2, K2, P2 *
Row 11: * P2, K2, P2 *	**Row 11:** * P2, K2, P2 *
Row 12: * K2, P2, K2 *	**Row 12:** * P2, K2, P2 *

CUT DIAGONALS

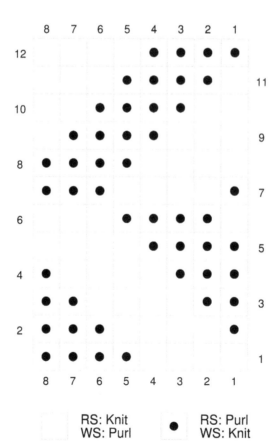

	8	7	6	5	4	3	2	1	
12					●	●	●	●	
					●	●	●	●	11
10			●	●	●	●			
		●	●	●	●				9
8	●	●	●	●					
	●	●	●					●	7
6				●	●	●	●	●	
					●	●	●	●	5
4	●					●	●	●	
	●	●					●	●	3
2	●	●	●					●	
	●	●	●	●					1
	8	7	6	5	4	3	2	1	

	RS: Knit WS: Purl	●	RS: Purl WS: Knit

CUT DIAGONALS

CAST ON

Multiples of 8

FLAT

Row 1: * K4, P4 *

Row 2: * K3, P4, K1 *

Row 3: * P2, K4, P2 *

Row 4: * K1, P4, K3 *

Row 5: * P4, K4 *

Row 6: * P3, K4, P1 *

Row 7: * P1, K4, P3 *

Row 8: * K4, P4 *

Row 9: * K3, P4, K1 *

Row 10: * P2, K4, P2 *

Row 11: * K1, P4, K3 *

Row 12: * P4, K4 *

IN THE ROUND

Row 1: * K4, P4 *

Row 2: * P1, K4, P3 *

Row 3: * P2, K4, P2 *

Row 4: * P3, K4, P1 *

Row 5: * P4, K4 *

Row 6: * K1, P4, K3 *

Row 7: * P1, K4, P3 *

Row 8: * K4, P4 *

Row 9: * K3, P4, K1 *

Row 10: * K2, P4, K2 *

Row 11: * K1, P4, K3 *

Row 12: * P4, K4 *

PIQUE TRIANGLE

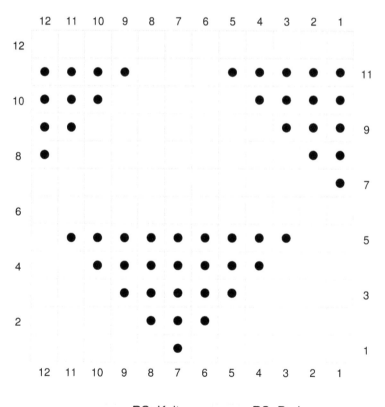

RS: Knit
WS: Purl

● RS: Purl
WS: Knit

PIQUE TRIANGLE

CAST ON

Multiples of 12

FLAT	IN THE ROUND
Row 1: * K6, P1, K5 *	**Row 1:** * K6, P1, K5 *
Row 2: * P4, K3, P5 *	**Row 2:** * K5, P3, K4 *
Row 3: * K4, P5, K3 *	**Row 3:** * K4, P5, K3 *
Row 4: * P2, K7, P3 *	**Row 4:** * K3, P7, K2 *
Row 5: * K2, P9, K1 *	**Row 5:** * K2, P9, K1 *
Row 6: * P12 *	**Row 6:** * K12 *
Row 7: * P1, K11 *	**Row 7:** * P1, K11 *
Row 8: * K1, P9, K2 *	**Row 8:** * P2, K9, P1 *
Row 9: * P3, K7, P2 *	**Row 9:** * P3, K7, P2 *
Row 10: * K3, P5, K4 *	**Row 10:** * P4, K5, P3 *
Row 11: * P5, K3, P4 *	**Row 11:** * P5, K3, P4 *
Row 12: * P12 *	**Row 12:** * K12 *

BASKET LOOP

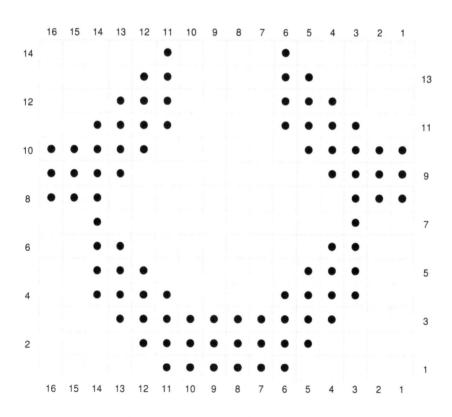

RS: Knit
WS: Purl

● RS: Purl
WS: Knit

BASKET LOOP

CAST ON

Multiples of 16

FLAT

Row 1: * K5, P6, K5 *
Row 2: * P4, K8, P4 *
Row 3: * K3, P10, K3 *
Row 4: * P2, K4, P4,
        K4, P2 *
Row 5: * K2, P3, K6,
        P3, K2 *
Row 6: * P2, K2, P8,
        K2, P2 *
Row 7: * K2, P1, K10,
        P1, K2 *
Row 8: * K3, P10, K3 *
Row 9: * P4, K8, P4 *
Row 10: * K5, P6, K5 *
Row 11: * K2, P4, K4,
         P4, K2 *
Row 12: * P3, K3, P4,
         K3, P3 *
Row 13: * K4, P2, K4,
         P2, K4 *
Row 14: * P5, K1, P4,
         K1, P5 *

IN THE ROUND

Row 1: * K5, P6, K5 *
Row 2: * K4, P8, K4 *
Row 3: * K3, P10, K3 *
Row 4: * K2, P4, K4,
        P4, K2 *
Row 5: * K2, P3, K6,
        P3, K2 *
Row 6: * K2, P2, K8,
        P2, K2 *
Row 7: * K2, P1, K10,
        P1, K2 *
Row 8: * P3, K10, P3 *
Row 9: * P4, K8, P4 *
Row 10: * P5, K6, P5 *
Row 11: * K2, P4, K4,
         P4, K2 *
Row 12: * K3, P3, K4,
         P3, K3 *
Row 13: * K4, P2, K4,
         P2, K4 *
Row 14: * K5, P1, K4,
         P1, K5 *

GARTER CHECKERBOARD

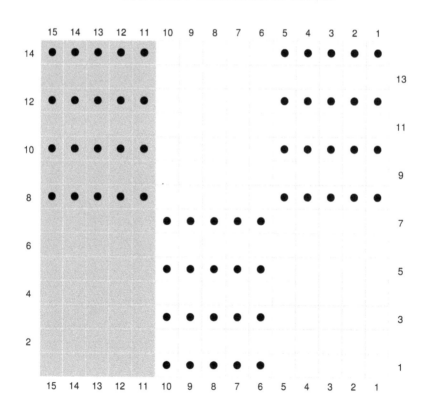

| | 15 | 14 | 13 | 12 | 11 | 10 | 9 | 8 | 7 | 6 | 5 | 4 | 3 | 2 | 1 | |

RS: Knit / WS: Purl ☐   ● RS: Purl / WS: Knit

GARTER CHECKERBOARD

CAST ON

Multiples of 10, plus 5

FLAT	**IN THE ROUND**
Row 1: * <u>K5, P5</u> *, K5	**Row 1:** * <u>K5, P5</u> *, K5
Row 2: Purl All	**Row 2:** Knit All
Row 3: * <u>K5, P5</u> *, K5	**Row 3:** * <u>K5, P5</u> *, K5
Row 4: Purl All	**Row 4:** Knit All
Row 5: * <u>K5, P5</u> *, K5	**Row 5:** * <u>K5, P5</u> *, K5
Row 6: Purl All	**Row 6:** Knit All
Row 7: * <u>K5, P5</u> *, K5	**Row 7:** * <u>K5, P5</u> *, K5
Row 8: K5, * <u>P5, K5</u> *	**Row 8:** * <u>P5, K5</u> *, P5
Row 9: Knit All	**Row 9:** Knit All
Row 10: K5, * <u>P5, K5</u> *	**Row 10:** * <u>P5, K5</u> *, P5
Row 11: Knit All	**Row 11:** Knit All
Row 12: K5, * <u>P5, K5</u> *	**Row 12:** * <u>P5, K5</u> *, P5
Row 13: Knit All	**Row 13:** Knit All
Row 14: K5, * <u>P5, K5</u> *	**Row 14:** * <u>P5, K5</u> *, P5

WINDOW STITCH

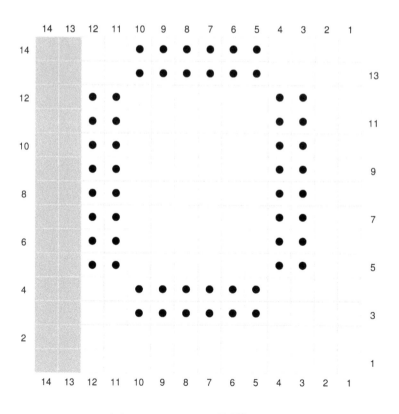

RS: Knit
WS: Purl

● RS: Purl
WS: Knit

WINDOW STITCH

CAST ON

Multiples of 12, plus 2

FLAT

Row 1: Knit All

Row 2: Purl All

Row 3: * K4, P6, K2 *, K2

Row 4: P2, * P2, K6, P4 *

Row 5: * K2, P2, K6, P2 *, K2

Row 6: P2, * K2, P6, K2, P2 *

Row 7: * K2, P2, K6, P2 *, K2

Row 8: P2, * K2, P6, K2, P2 *

Row 9: * K2, P2, K6, P2 *, K2

Row 10: P2, * K2, P6, K2, P2 *

Row 11: * K2, P2, K6, P2 *, K2

Row 12: P2, * K2, P6, K2, P2 *

Row 13: * K4, P6, K2 *, K2

Row 14: P2, * P2, K6, P4 *

IN THE ROUND

Row 1: Knit All

Row 2: Knit All

Row 3: * K4, P6, K2 *, K2

Row 4: * K4, P6, K2 *, K2

Row 5: * K2, P2, K6, P2 *, K2

Row 6: * K2, P2, K6, P2 *, K2

Row 7: * K2, P2, K6, P2 *, K2

Row 8: * K2, P2, K6, P2 *, K2

Row 9: * K2, P2, K6, P2 *, K2

Row 10: * K2, P2, K6, P2 *, K2

Row 11: * K2, P2, K6, P2 *, K2

Row 12: * K2, P2, K6, P2 *, K2

Row 13: * K4, P6, K2 *, K2

Row 14: * K4, P6, K2 *, K2

DIAGONAL ZIGZAG

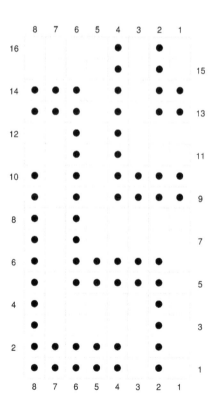

	RS: Knit		
	WS: Purl	●	RS: Purl WS: Knit

DIAGONAL ZIGZAG

CAST ON

Multiples of 8

FLAT

Row 1: * K1, P1, K1, P5 *
Row 2: * K5, P1, K1, P1 *
Row 3: * K1, P1, K5, P1 *
Row 4: * K1, P5, K1, P1 *
Row 5: * K1, P5, K1, P1 *
Row 6: * K1, P1, K5, P1 *
Row 7: * K5, P1, K1, P1 *
Row 8: * K1, P1, K1, P5 *
Row 9: * P4, K1, P1,
K1, P1 *
Row 10: * K1, P1, K1,
P1, K4 *
Row 11: * K3, P1, K1,
P1, K2 *
Row 12: * P2, K1, P1,
K1, P3 *
Row 13: * P2, K1, P1,
K1, P3 *
Row 14: * K3, P1, K1,
P1, K2 *
Row 15: * K1, P1, K1,
P1, K4 *
Row 16: * P4, K1, P1,
K1, P1 *

IN THE ROUND

Row 1: * K1, P1, K1, P5 *
Row 2: * K1, P1, K1, P5 *
Row 3: * K1, P1, K5, P1 *
Row 4: * K1, P1, K5, P1 *
Row 5: * K1, P5, K1, P1 *
Row 6: * K1, P5, K1, P1 *
Row 7: * K5, P1, K1, P1 *
Row 8: * K5, P1, K1, P1 *
Row 9: * P4, K1, P1,
K1, P1 *
Row 10: * P4, K1, P1,
K1, P1 *
Row 11: * K3, P1, K1,
P1, K2 *
Row 12: * K3, P1, K1,
P1, K2 *
Row 13: * P2, K1, P1,
K1, P3 *
Row 14: * P2, K1, P1,
K1, P3 *
Row 15: * K1, P1, K1,
P1, K4 *
Row 16: * K1, P1, K1,
P1, K4 *

FANCY DIAMOND

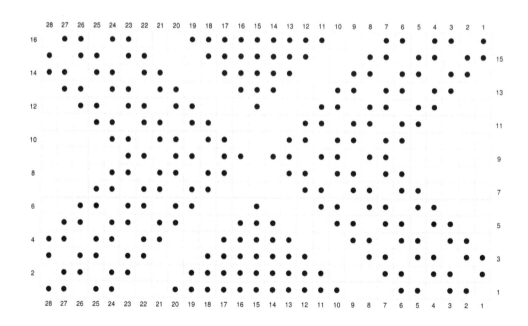

RS: Knit
WS: Purl

● RS: Purl
WS: Knit

FANCY DIAMOND

CAST ON

Multiples of 28

FLAT

Row 1: * K1, P2, K1, P2, K3, P11, K3, P2, K1, P2 *

Row 2 & 16: * P1, K2, P1, K2, P3, K9, P3, K2, P1, K2, P1, K1 *

Row 3 & 15: * P2, K1, P2, K1, P2, K3, P7, K3, P2, K1, P2, K1, P1 *

Row 4 & 14: * K2, P1, K2, P1, K2, P3, K5, P3, K2, P1, K2, P1, K2, P1 *

Row 5 & 13: * K2, P2, K1, P2, K1, P2, K3, P3, K3, P2, K1, P2, K1, P2, K1 *

Row 6 & 12: * P2, K2, P1, K2, P1, K2, P3, K1, P3, K2, P1, K2, P1, K2, P3 *

Row 7 & 11: * K4, P2, K1, P2, K1, P2, K5, P2, K1, P2, K1, P2, K3 *

Row 8 & 10: * P4, K2, P1, K2, P1, K2, P3, K2, P1, K2, P1, K2, P5 *

Row 9: * K6, P2, K1, P2, K1, P2, K1, P2, K1, P2, K1, P2, K5 *

IN THE ROUND

Row 1: * K1, P2, K1, P2, K3, P11, K3, P2, K1, P2 *

Row 2 & 16: * P1, K1, P2, K1, P2, K3, P9, K3, P2, K1, P2, K1 *

Row 3 & 15: * P2, K1, P2, K1, P2, K3, P7, K3, P2, K1, P2, K1, P1 *

Row 4 & 14: * K1, P2, K1, P2, K1, P2, K3, P5, K3, P2, K1, P2, K1, P2 *

Row 5 & 13: * K2, P2, K1, P2, K1, P2, K3, P3, K3, P2, K1, P2, K, P2, K1 *

Row 6 & 12: * K3, P2, K1, P2, K1, P2, K3, P1, K3, P2, K1, P2, K1, P2, K2 *

Row 7 & 11: * K4, P2, K1, P2, K1, P2, K5, P2, K1, P2, K1, P2, K3 *

Row 8 & 10: * K5, P2, K1, P2, K1, P2, K3, P2, K1, P2, K1, P2, K4 *

Row 9: * K6, P2, K1, P2, K1, P2, K1, P2, K1, P2, K1, P2, K5 *

EMBOSSED LEAF

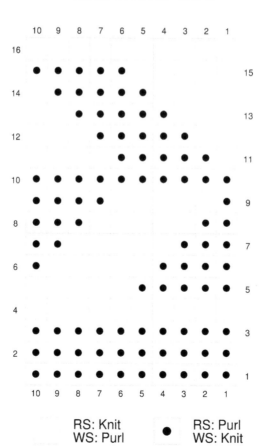

RS: Knit
WS: Purl

● RS: Purl
WS: Knit

EMBOSSED LEAF

CAST ON

Multiples of 10

FLAT	IN THE ROUND
Row 1: Purl All	**Row 1:** Purl All
Row 2: Knit All	**Row 2:** Purl All
Row 3: Purl All	**Row 3:** Purl All
Row 4: Purl All	**Row 4:** Knit All
Row 5: * P5, K5 *	**Row 5:** * P5, K5 *
Row 6: * K1, P5, K4 *	**Row 6:** * P4, K5, P1 *
Row 7: * P3, K5, P2 *	**Row 7:** * P3, K5, P2 *
Row 8: * K3, P5, K2 *	**Row 8:** * P2, K5, P3 *
Row 9: * P1, K5, P4 *	**Row 9:** * P1, K5, P4 *
Row 10: Knit All	**Row 10:** Purl All
Row 11: * K1, P5, K4 *	**Row 11:** * K1, P5, K4 *
Row 12: * P3, K5, P2 *	**Row 12:** * K2, P5, K3 *
Row 13: * K3, P5, K2 *	**Row 13:** * K3, P5, K2 *
Row 14: * P1, K5, P4 *	**Row 14:** * K4, P5, K1 *
Row 15: * K5, P5 *	**Row 15:** * K5, P5 *
Row 16: Purl All	**Row 16:** Knit All

PARALLELOGRAM STITCH

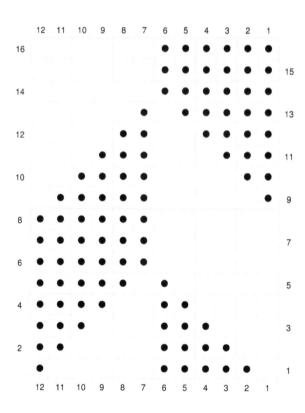

RS: Knit
WS: Purl

● RS: Purl
WS: Knit

PARALLELOGRAM STITCH

CAST ON

Multiples of 12

FLAT

Row 1: * K1, P5, K5, P1 *

Row 2: * K2, P4, K4, P2 *

Row 3: * K3, P3 *

Row 4: * K4, P2, K2, P4 *

Row 5: * K5, P1, K1, P5 *

Row 6: * K6, P6 *

Row 7: * K6, P6 *

Row 8: * K6, P6 *

Row 9: * P1, K5, P5, K1 *

Row 10: * P2, K4, P4, K2 *

Row 11: * P3, K3 *

Row 12: * P4, K2, P2, K4 *

Row 13: * P5, K1, P1, K5 *

Row 14: * P6, K6 *

Row 15: * P6, K6 *

Row 16: * P6, K6 *

IN THE ROUND

Row 1: * K1, P5, K5, P1 *

Row 2: * K2, P4, K4, P2 *

Row 3: * K3, P3 *

Row 4: * K4, P2, K2, P4 *

Row 5: * K5, P1, K1, P5 *

Row 6: * K6, P6 *

Row 7: * K6, P6 *

Row 8: * K6, P6 *

Row 9: * P1, K5, P5, K1 *

Row 10: * P2, K4, P4, K2 *

Row 11: * P3, K3 *

Row 12: * P4, K2, P2, K4 *

Row 13: * P5, K1, P1, K5 *

Row 14: * P6, K6 *

Row 15: * P6, K6 *

Row 16: * P6, K6 *

18 to 28-ROW REPEATS

DIAGONAL SPIRAL RIB

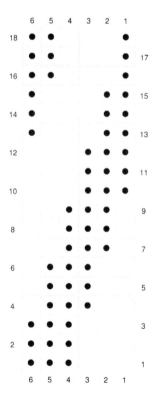

RS: Knit
WS: Purl

● RS: Purl
WS: Knit

DIAGONAL SPIRAL RIB

CAST ON

Multiples of 6

FLAT	IN THE ROUND
Row 1: * K3, P3 *	**Row 1:** * K3, P3 *
Row 2: * K3, P3 *	**Row 2:** * K3, P3 *
Row 3: * K3, P3 *	**Row 3:** * K3, P3 *
Row 4: * P1, K3, P2 *	**Row 4:** * K2, P3, K1 *
Row 5: * K2, P3, K1 *	**Row 5:** * K2, P3, K1 *
Row 6: * P1, K3, P2 *	**Row 6:** * K2, P3, K1 *
Row 7: * K1, P3, K2 *	**Row 7:** * K1, P3, K2 *
Row 8: * P2, K3, P1 *	**Row 8:** * K1, P3, K2 *
Row 9: * K1, P3, K2 *	**Row 9:** * K1, P3, K2 *
Row 10: * P3, K3 *	**Row 10:** * P3, K3 *
Row 11: * P3, K3 *	**Row 11:** * P3, K3 *
Row 12: * P3, K3 *	**Row 12:** * P3, K3 *
Row 13: * P2, K3, P1 *	**Row 13:** * P2, K3, P1 *
Row 14: * K1, P3, K2 *	**Row 14:** * P2, K3, P1 *
Row 15: * P2, K3, P1 *	**Row 15:** * P2, K3, P1 *
Row 16: * K2, P3, K1 *	**Row 16:** * P1, K3, P2 *
Row 17: * P1, K3, P2 *	**Row 17:** * P1, K3, P2 *
Row 18: * K2, P3, K1 *	**Row 18:** * P1, K3, P2 *

LATTICE WITH SEED

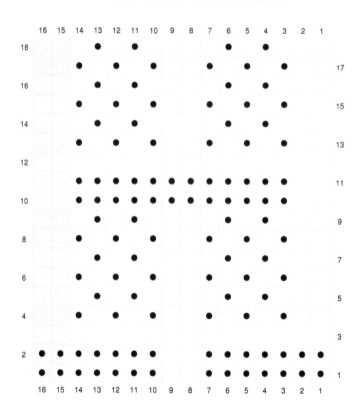

RS: Knit
WS: Purl

● RS: Purl
WS: Knit

LATTICE
WITH SEED

CAST ON

Multiples of 14, plus 2

FLAT

Row 1: * P7, K2, P5 *, P2
Row 2: K2, * K5, P2, K7 *
Row 3: Knit All
Row 4: P2, * K1, P1, K1, P1, K1, P2 *
Row 5: * K3, P1, K1, P1, K4, P1, K1, P1, K1 *, K2
Row 6: P2, * K1, P1, K1, P1, K1, P2 *
Row 7: * K3, P1, K1, P1, K4, P1, K1, P1, K1 *, K2
Row 8: P2, * K1, P1, K1, P1, K1, P2 *
Row 9: * K3, P1, K1, P1, K4, P1, K1, P1, K1 *, K2
Row 10: P2, * K12, P2 *
Row 11: * K2, P12 *, K2
Row 12: Purl All
Row 13: * K2, P1, K1, P1, K1, P1 *, K2
Row 14: P2, * P1, K1, P1, K1, P4, K1, P1, K1, P3 *
Row 15: * K2, P1, K1, P1, K1, P1 *, K2
Row 16: P2, * P1, K1, P1, K1, P4, K1, P1, K1, P3 *
Row 17: * K2, P1, K1, P1, K1, P1 *, K2
Row 18: P2, * P1, K1, P1, K1, P4, K1, P1, K1, P3 *

IN THE ROUND

Row 1: * P7, K2, P5 *, P2
Row 2: * P7, K2, P5 *, P2
Row 3: Knit All
Row 4: * K2, P1, K1, P1, K1, P1 *, K2
Row 5: * K3, P1, K1, P1, K4, P1, K1, P1, K1 *, K2
Row 6: * K2, P1, K1, P1, K1, P1 *, K2
Row 7: * K3, P1, K1, P1, K4, P1, K1, P1, K1 *, K2
Row 8: * K2, P1, K1, P1, K1, P1 *, K2
Row 9: * K3, P1, K1, P1, K4, P1, K1, P1, K1 *, K2
Row 10: * K2, P12 *, K2
Row 11: * K2, P12 *, K2
Row 12: Knit All
Row 13: * K2, P1, K1, P1, K1, P1 *, K2
Row 14: * K3, P1, K1, P1, K4, P1, K1, P1, K1 *, K2
Row 15: * K2, P1, K1, P1, K1, P1 *, K2
Row 16: * K3, P1, K1, P1, K4, P1, K1, P1, K1 *, K2
Row 17: * K2, P1, K1, P1, K1, P1 *, K2
Row 18: * K3, P1, K1, P1, K4, P1, K1, P1, K1 *, K2

WIDE CHEVRON ZIGZAG

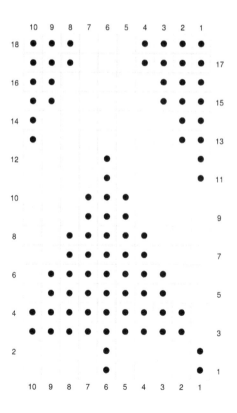

| | RS: Knit | • | RS: Purl |
| | WS: Purl | | WS: Knit |

WIDE CHEVRON
ZIGZAG

CAST ON

Multiples of 10

FLAT	IN THE ROUND
Row 1: * P1, K4 *	**Row 1:** * P1, K4 *
Row 2: * P4, K1 *	**Row 2:** * P1, K4 *
Row 3: * K1, P9 *	**Row 3:** * K1, P9 *
Row 4: * P9, K1 *	**Row 4:** * K1, P9 *
Row 5: * K2, P7, K1 *	**Row 5:** * K2, P7, K1 *
Row 6: * P1, K7, P2 *	**Row 6:** * K2, P7, K1 *
Row 7: * K3, P5, K2 *	**Row 7:** * K3, P5, K2 *
Row 8: * P2, K5, P3 *	**Row 8:** * K3, P5, K2 *
Row 9: * K4, P3, K3 *	**Row 9:** * K4, P3, K3 *
Row 10: * P3, K3, P4 *	**Row 10:** * K4, P3, K3 *
Row 11: * P1, K4 *	**Row 11:** * P1, K4 *
Row 12: * P4, K1 *	**Row 12:** * P1, K4 *
Row 13: * P2, K7, P1 *	**Row 13:** * P2, K7, P1 *
Row 14: * K1, P7, K2 *	**Row 14:** * P2, K7, P1 *
Row 15: * P3, K5, P2 *	**Row 15:** * P3, K5, P2 *
Row 16: * K2, P5, K3 *	**Row 16:** * P3, K5, P2 *
Row 17: * P4, K3, P3 *	**Row 17:** * P4, K3, P3 *
Row 18: * K3, P3, K4 *	**Row 18:** * P4, K3, P3 *

TUMBLING MOSS BLOCKS

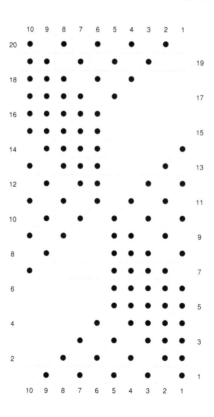

RS: Knit
WS: Purl

● RS: Purl
WS: Knit

TUMBLING MOSS BLOCKS

CAST ON

Multiples of 10

FLAT

Row 1: * P1, K1 *
Row 2: * P2, K1, P1, K1, P1, K1, P1, K2 *
Row 3: * P3, K1, P1, K1, P1, K3 *
Row 4: * P4, K1, P1, K4 *
Row 5: * P5, K5 *
Row 6: * P5, K5 *
Row 7: * K1, P4, K4, P1 *
Row 8: * P1, K1, P3, K3, P1, K1 *
Row 9: * K1, P1, K1, P2, K2, P1, K1, P1 *
Row 10: * P1, K1 *
Row 11: * K1, P1 *
Row 12: * P1, K1, P1, K2, P2, K1, P1, K1 *
Row 13: * K1, P1, K3, P3, K1, P1 *
Row 14: * P1, K4, P4, K1 *
Row 15: * K5, P5 *
Row 16: * K5, P5 *
Row 17: * K4, P1, K1, P4 *
Row 18: * K3, P1, K1, P1, K1, P3 *
Row 19: * K2, P1, K1, P1, K1, P1, K1, P2 *
Row 20: * K1, P1 *

IN THE ROUND

Row 1: * P1, K1 *
Row 2: * P2, K1, P1, K1, P1, K1, P1, K2 *
Row 3: * P3, K1, P1, K1, P1, K3 *
Row 4: * P4, K1, P1, K4 *
Row 5: * P5, K5 *
Row 6: * P5, K5 *
Row 7: * K1, P4, K4, P1 *
Row 8: * P1, K1, P3, K3, P1, K1 *
Row 9: * K1, P1, K1, P2, K2, P1, K1, P1 *
Row 10: * P1, K1 *
Row 11: * K1, P1 *
Row 12: * P1, K1, P1, K2, P2, K1, P1, K1 *
Row 13: * K1, P1, K3, P3, K1, P1 *
Row 14: * P1, K4, P4, K1 *
Row 15: * K5, P5 *
Row 16: * K5, P5 *
Row 17: * K4, P1, K1, P4 *
Row 18: * K3, P1, K1, P1, K1, P3 *
Row 19: * K2, P1, K1, P1, K1, P1, K1, P2 *
Row 20: * K1, P1 *

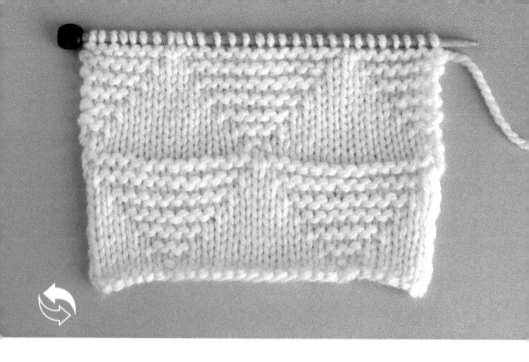

LARGE TRIANGLES

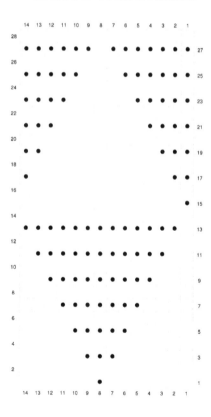

	RS: Knit		RS: Purl
	WS: Purl	●	WS: Knit

LARGE TRIANGLES

CAST ON

Multiples of 14

FLAT

Row 1: * K7, P1, K6 *
Row 2: Purl All
Row 3: * K6, P3 K5 *
Row 4: Purl All
Row 5: * K5, P5, K4 *
Row 6: Purl All
Row 7: * K4 P7, K3 *
Row 8: Purl All
Row 9: * K3, P9, K2 *
Row 10: Purl All
Row 11: * K2, P11, K1 *
Row 12: Purl All
Row 13: * K1, P13 *
Row 14: Purl All
Row 15: * P1, K13 *
Row 16: Purl All
Row 17: * P2, K11, P1 *
Row 18: Purl All
Row 19: * P3, K9, P2 *
Row 20: Purl All
Row 21: * P4, K7, P3 *
Row 22: Purl All
Row 23: * P5, K5, P4 *
Row 24: Purl All
Row 25: * P6, K3, P5 *
Row 26: Purl All
Row 27: * P7, K1, P6 *
Row 28: Purl All

IN THE ROUND

Row 1: * K7, P1, K6 *
Row 2: Knit All
Row 3: * K6, P3 K5 *
Row 4: Knit All
Row 5: * K5, P5, K4 *
Row 6: Knit All
Row 7: * K4 P7, K3 *
Row 8: Knit All
Row 9: * K3, P9, K2 *
Row 10: Knit All
Row 11: * K2, P11, K1 *
Row 12: Knit All
Row 13: * K1, P13 *
Row 14: Knit All
Row 15: * P1, K13 *
Row 16: Knit All
Row 17: * P2, K11, P1 *
Row 18: Knit All
Row 19: * P3, K9, P2 *
Row 20: Knit All
Row 21: * P4, K7, P3 *
Row 22: Knit All
Row 23: * P5, K5, P4 *
Row 24: Knit All
Row 25: * P6, K3, P5 *
Row 26: Knit All
Row 27: * P7, K1, P6 *
Row 28: Knit All

Lightning Source UK Ltd.
Milton Keynes UK
UKHW020243050322
399582UK00006B/225